ROCK & ROLL HALL OF FAMERS

The Rolling Stones

THOMAS FORGET

To my father Gerry, the original Street Fighting Man

Published in 2003 by The Rosen Publishing Group, Inc.
29 East 21st Street, New York, NY 10010

Copyright © 2003 by The Rosen Publishing Group, Inc.

First Edition

All rights reserved. No part of this book may be reproduced in any form without permission in writing from the publisher, except by a reviewer.

Library of Congress Cataloging-in-Publication Data

Forget, Thomas.
The Rolling Stones / by Thomas Forget.— 1st ed.
p. cm. — (Rock & roll hall of famers)
Includes discography (p.   ), list of Web sites (p.   ),
bibliographical references (p.   ), and index.
ISBN: 978-1-4358-8910-1
1. Rolling Stones—Juvenile literature. 2. Rock musicians—Biography—Juvenile literature. [1. Rolling Stones. 2. Musicians. 3. Rock music.] I. Title. II. Series.
ML3930.R64 F67 2002
782.42166'092'2—dc21

2001008156

Manufactured in the United States of America

CONTENTS

Introduction	5
1. From Pebbles to Stones	9
2. On a Roll	22
3. Stone's Throw from Stardom	34
4. Stones on Top	50
5. The Exiles	67
6. Start Up the Eighties	80
7. Satisfaction	91
Selected Discography	103
Glossary	104
To Find Out More	106
For Further Reading	108
Index	109

The Rolling Stones are considered by many to be the greatest rock and roll band of all time.

Introduction

There's a vampire playing guitar, zombies on the drums and bass, a wild furry animal playing the other guitar, and a savage howling the vocals. If you were a parent in the 1960s, this may well have been your view of London's notorious Rolling Stones. If you were a teen, however, you would have seen freedom—freedom from school, work, and parents. You would have felt empowered to miss a haircut, to wear your pants tight, or to

The Rolling Stones

dance with someone. For many teens, the Rolling Stones brought an alternative to the monotony of middle-class life.

Mick Jagger, Keith Richards, Brian Jones, Bill Wyman, and Charlie Watts were just a group of middle-class English boys who loved American rock and roll and blues, and knew for certain they were not made for the nine-to-five life. While they went on to become millionaires, the teens at the time felt that they could relate to the Rolling Stones. The Stones were the new spokesmen for youth culture.

Parents, politicians, priests, the police, and even other rockers saw things a little differently. The Stones rubbed anyone over thirty the wrong way. Glyn Johns, an engineer who frequently worked with the band, said, "It was just their appearance, their clothes, their hair, their whole attitude was immediately obvious to you as soon as you saw them playing. It was just a complete 'pppprt' to society and everybody and anything." Their early shows almost routinely turned into riots. They were banned from concert halls, thrown out of hotels, and asked not to return to

Introduction

While cultivating the image of notorious bad boys, the Stones have also created a widely respected body of music.

restaurants. Through it all, however, a strange thing started to happen. The Rolling Stones, Jagger and Richards in particular, found themselves strengthening as songwriters and artists, and they eventually achieved levels of popularity and respectability reserved for society's most beloved entertainers. Explosions of youth energy and frustration powered the

The Rolling Stones

Stones to the top of the charts. Talent and intelligence kept them there and allowed them to become the elder statesmen of rock. They have even surpassed their spiritual brothers, the Beatles, by staying together over thirty-one years after the Beatles called it quits.

The Rolling Stones have been playing it hard and loud for forty years and still don't seem to know how to stop. Rising during the British pop invasion, they have weathered the storms of popular culture like no act in history. The Stones have somehow managed to successfully navigate through every single fleeting trend in pop music, and have even brought new fans of every age and generation on board with them.

They don't just play rock and roll; the Rolling Stones ARE rock and roll, so it's most fitting that they sit pretty among the ranks of Rock and Roll Hall of Famers. The story of how they got to that cushy position from the gray streets of post-war London is a long one, and their history is now looked at as the stuff of legend.

1

From Pebbles to Stones

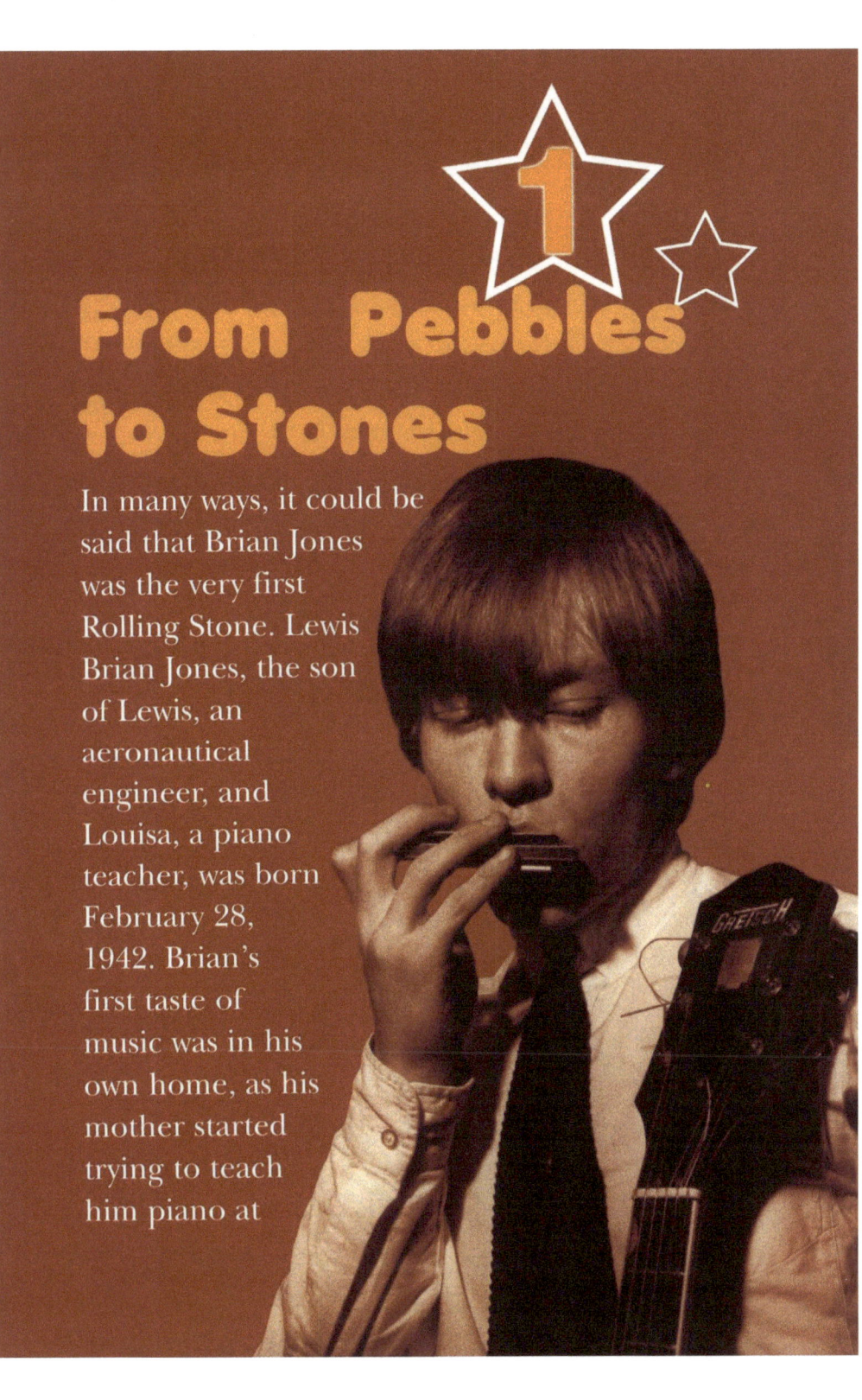

In many ways, it could be said that Brian Jones was the very first Rolling Stone. Lewis Brian Jones, the son of Lewis, an aeronautical engineer, and Louisa, a piano teacher, was born February 28, 1942. Brian's first taste of music was in his own home, as his mother started trying to teach him piano at

The Rolling Stones

age six. Though Brian kept at it until he was fourteen, he showed little interest in music at all. Little interest, that is, until he started playing the clarinet. Brian had asthma (a condition that affected his ability to breathe properly), but he didn't let that stop him. In a short time, he developed an obsession with jazz music and was driving his parents crazy with loud jazz records. To them, it sounded like noise, but to Brian, it was becoming the only thing that mattered.

Surrendering to the Music

As time passed, it became very clear to everybody that Brian Jones was not your average young Englishman. He hated school and wanted no part of what he saw as a boring, middle-class English life. In his late teens, he abandoned the ideas of school and work, and decided to give himself over fully to music.

In addition to his clarinet, Brian had begun playing the guitar. Not only was he obsessed with jazz, but he had also begun what would become a long relationship with American rhythm and

From Pebbles to Stones

blues (R & B). He spent hours practicing the music of Muddy Waters, Howlin' Wolf, and other American blues masters.

By age twenty, Brian already had a child and live-in girlfriend to support. Times were hard, but he knew what was important to him. He began sitting in and jamming with local R & B musicians, most of whom were blown away by his talent. One of those musicians, Alexis Korner, introduced Brian to a couple of other young musicians. Their names were Michael Jagger and Keith Richards. Though some would argue otherwise, Brian had little idea at the time how intertwined their lives would become.

The Glimmer Twins

Keith Richards was a suburban youth who knew he belonged somewhere else. Born in Dartford, England, on December 18, 1943, Keith had music in his blood. His mother played piano, and her father, Gus Dupree, had led a dance band in the 1930s. It was his grandfather's guitar that Keith first toyed with. Keith, like

The Rolling Stones

A young Keith Richards at the Richmond Jazz Festival in 1964

Brian Jones, hated school. At technical school, Keith found himself struggling through classes. His lack of motivation led to Keith's expulsion from school in his fourth year.

Around this time, rock and roll started to make its assault on English soil. Keith liked what he heard, and he started to get the idea that there was something he could do with his interest in music. Like so many other teens, he was captivated by Elvis Presley. Keith recalled, "The first record that really turned me on out of the Rock and Roll thing was 'Heartbreak Hotel.'" In addition to Elvis, Richards grew to deeply love the raw rock sounds of Chuck Berry.

Keith found rock and roll, but he had to find himself a niche in life. The school that kicked him

From Pebbles to Stones

out found him a place in an art school. Art school turned out to be a haven for musicians. Keith met and started playing with a young guitarist named Dick Taylor, and the two of them jammed with whomever they could.

At the beginning of Keith's last year of art school, he had a chance meeting with someone from his past. Before he went on to technical school, Keith had had a schoolmate from Dartford named Michael Jagger, whom everyone called Mick. Mick Jagger was born on July 26, 1943. His father was a physical education teacher from Dartford, so he became interested in athletics. By age twelve, Mick was teaching games to kids on an American army base. It was there that Mick was first exposed to the blues,

Dick Taylor *(left)* of the Pretty Things, was the Rolling Stones' first bassist.

The Rolling Stones

through one of the cooks at the base. Falling in love with the rhythms of this music was typical of British teens at that time.

Mick went on to a different school than Keith, and they lost touch. Their next meeting did not occur until they were both seventeen. Mick was attending the London School of Economics. When he and Keith ran into each other at the Dartford train station, he was carrying some American R & B records, including Chuck Berry. The boys hit it off instantly.

As it turned out, Mick knew Keith's school friend Dick Taylor. The three of them started practicing together. Mick played the harmonica and sang, and Keith and Dick strummed their guitars. Meeting Mick exposed Keith to many new sounds. Mick had a large collection of records from America, and he was excited to share his world with his new friend.

Getting It Together

Around the time that Mick and Keith reconnected, a British musician named Alexis

From Pebbles to Stones

Korner was starting to make the scene. He had recently started a band with some local rockers, including a drummer named Charlie Watts. One night when Mick and Keith went out to see Alex's band play, he had a guest guitarist sit in. They were instantly blown away by the guitarist's rendition of bluesman Elmore James's "Dust My Broom." The guitarist was Brian Jones.

After the show, Mick and Keith got to talking with

Fun Fact!

At the beginning of their live music career, Mick Jagger had so little room to move on the small stages of the venues they played that he had to create some strange dances all his own. Later, as the band gained popularity, he worked the moves into his special trademark dancing. Jagger's often-imitated hip swinging and jerking around are still present in his performances to this day.

Brian Jones *(left)* **and Keith Richards jam together in December 1963.**

From Pebbles to Stones

Brian. He was eager to get to London, where he could play his guitar to his heart's content. It was clear from the start that Brian, Mick, and Keith would be playing together, and in no time they were all playing with Alexis Korner. In May 1962, a local music paper, *Disc*, even ran an article, "Singer Joins Korner," that spoke of Mick's Thursday and Saturday night stands with the band.

Brian, however, was not content just playing occasionally, and he decided to start his own group. Keith wasted no time in reporting to Brian's rehearsals. And another man, Ian "Stu" Stewart, answered an ad Brian placed and came to play the piano. Stu was a boogie-woogie-style piano player from Scotland, and he loved rock and roll because it gave him the opportunity to play as hard as he liked.

Keith spoke to Mick, and pretty soon he was a part of Brian Jones's new rock outfit. At that point it was Brian, Mick, Keith, Stu, and Keith's old friend Dick Taylor. They had two guitars, a bass, a piano, and a singer who also played harmonica. They were still in need of a drummer, but they had become a band, and things were starting to gel.

The Rolling Stones

Rhythm Section Wanted

Alexis Korner, one of the first musicians with whom the original Rolling Stones played

In the winter of 1962, the boys were getting things together, but they were broke. Mick was still in school, just in case his dreams of becoming a popular musician didn't work out. Brian was working in a record store and trying to support a child. Keith wasn't working at all and was staying with Brian. They had picked up a mediocre drummer named Tony Chapman, and Dick Taylor was playing the bass for them, but they needed people that could match their talent.

Alexis Korner's band was offered a steady job playing on the British Broadcasting Company (BBC). They had been playing at the Marquee

From Pebbles to Stones

Jazz Club in London on Thursdays and would have to give up this gig, so Alexis offered Brian's band his slot. Now that the band actually had a paying gig, they needed a name. Brian Jones once again looked to the blues for inspiration. He thought of the Muddy Waters song "Mannish Boy." In the song, there is a line that talks about a "Rollin' Stone." When *Disc* ran the first article ever mentioning the band on July 7, 1962, however, they were referred to as Mick Jagger and the Rolling Stones. From then on, they were the Rolling Stones, and nothing was going to stop them from rolling now that they were on their way.

The Rolling Stones

1962
Brian Jones founds the Rolling Stones. Along for the ride are Mick Jagger, Ian Stewart, and Keith Richards, who will stay with the band (in some form or another) for years.

1963
In January, Brian, Mick, and Keith play their first show with Bill Wyman and Charlie Watts, making it the debut of the Stones lineup as most would come to know it.

1965
"Satisfaction" becomes the Rolling Stones' first number-one single in the United States.

1963
In May, the Rolling Stones sign a contract with Decca Records.

1964
The Rolling Stones release their self-titled, first full-length LP. It shoots to number one on the charts, ending the Beatles' year-long deadlock on the number-one position.

From Pebbles to Stones

1969
On July 2, Brian Jones is found dead in the swimming pool of his country house. On December 6, the Stones' 1969 tour comes to a tragic end with a show at San Francisco's Altamont Speedway, when a young man is stabbed to death by one of the Hell's Angels.

1971
The Stones release *Sticky Fingers*, their first album on their own label. It is successful both commercially and critically.

1974
Mick Taylor quits the Stones. He is replaced by Ron Wood, a veteran of the British rock scene. Wood remains with the group to this day.

1989
Pete Townshend of the Who inducts the Rolling Stones into the Rock and Roll Hall of Fame in Cleveland, Ohio.

2001
Mick Jagger and Keith Richards perform two songs at the Concert for New York, a benefit show for the families of the victims of September 11, 2001.

On a Roll

Brian's boys now had a name and a regular gig to cut their teeth on, but their lineup was still not as stable as they would have liked it to be. In September 1962, Dick Taylor left the group to study art, leaving them without a bassist. Brian, Mick, and Keith were living together in a dingy apartment, but Mick and Keith were glad to have finally left

On a Roll

their parents' homes. They were playing more, and their sound was getting better, but they needed to do something about their lack of a bass player before the band could do anything important.

A New Rolling Stone

Tony Chapman, their drummer, had been playing in another band called the Cliftons and said he knew a bassist who had his own equipment. He brought that friend, Bill Perks, to see the Stones play one day. Perks was older than the Stones, having been born in 1936, and was already married with a child. He had previously been a member of the Royal Air Force (RAF) and was working a day job at an engineering firm. As a musician, he had learned to play the clarinet and organ at a young age, and he had picked up bass guitar in the army while stationed in Germany.

When Perks came around to see the Stones, he struck up a conversation with Ian Stewart, and they discussed the band's need for a new bass player. Two days later, Perks went to a

The Rolling Stones

rehearsal at the Weatherby Arms pub. There was not much chemistry between Perks and the boys, but there was enough. Also, he got along well with Stu, as they were older (Stu was born in 1938) and quite a bit more conservative than Brian and the others. Perks began using the stage name Lee Whyman (after a friend from the RAF) and later changed it to Bill Wyman. In a short while, he was their new bassist. Now if only they had a better drummer . . .

Watts Happening

Ever since Brian had formed the band, he had been in hot pursuit of Charlie Watts. Charlie was a jazz drummer with Alex Korner's band. He was not into the blues or rock and roll like the rest of the Stones. He had started playing the drums at around age fourteen. His parents had bought him a banjo, which he turned into a drum by removing the neck of the instrument.

Like Bill Wyman, Charlie had a steady day job. He was a typesetter's assistant at a graphic design firm, and he had been able to make a

On a Roll

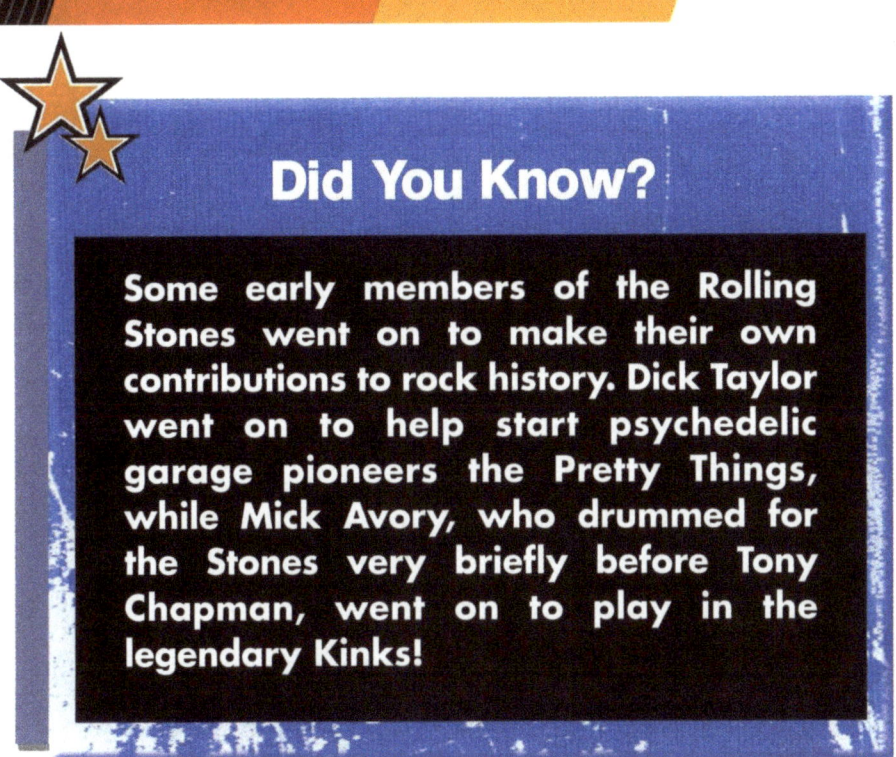

Did You Know?

Some early members of the Rolling Stones went on to make their own contributions to rock history. Dick Taylor went on to help start psychedelic garage pioneers the Pretty Things, while Mick Avory, who drummed for the Stones very briefly before Tony Chapman, went on to play in the legendary Kinks!

decent living thus far. He was also able to travel to places like Denmark as part of the job, so he was not in any hurry to stop working. Up to this point, playing the drums was mostly a hobby for him—but that would soon change.

The problem the Stones had was that they simply did not have the money to lure Watts away from the security of the nine-to-five life. Once

The Rolling Stones

The Stones play a television gig in the U.K. in October 1965.

they started playing on a more regular basis, they were finally able to offer Charlie twenty pounds (the equivalent to about $28.50) a week. It wasn't a lot, but it was enough for Charlie, and they soon found themselves with a highly skilled drummer.

Charlie's first gig with the Stones, on January 17, 1963, marked the first time Bill, Brian, Charlie,

On a Roll

Keith, and Mick played together. The band's lineup, which took such a long time to take proper shape, would stay this way for many years.

Stone Steady

Now that they had a lineup they were happy with, the Rolling Stones could get on with the business of conquering the pop world. They had already been playing the gig they inherited from Alexis Korner at the Marquee Jazz Club, but they quickly secured themselves another steady engagement at the Crawdaddy Club in the Richmond Station Hotel. This would be the first time that they would be exposed to an audience outside of the die-hard jazz fans that came to the Marquee.

Their live reputation began to spread like wildfire. The band was rehearsing and playing so often that they were becoming seasoned in the business of rock and roll. Said Ian Stewart of Keith and Brian, "There was never any suggestion of a lead and rhythm guitar player. They were two guitar players that were like someone's right and left hand." The rest of the band also found a

The Rolling Stones

comfortable groove, and it was clear that things were going to happen.

Enter Andrew

The publicity machine that powered the rise of the Beatles was made up of many parts. One small wheel in this machine was a young Englishman named Andrew Loog Oldham. The son of a working-class single mother, Andrew never met his father, who was killed in World War II. Growing up, Andrew never had much in the way of material possessions, and he used to dream that he was a character in a movie. He could feel the entertainment business in his bones, and he worked hard to sharpen his skills.

After years of private school, where he would talk his way in and out of trouble and scam older

Andrew Oldham, a former manager and promotor for the Stones

On a Roll

authorities for better television privileges, he worked a number of odd jobs related to the London club scene. Whether it was working in a bar or as a show promoter, Andrew believed that any job involved with entertainment was a job for him. He eventually found himself a job working in publicity with the Beatles' manager, Brian Epstein.

One day, Andrew received a call from a journalist telling him that he had to check out the Rolling Stones, a new band that people were buzzing about. Andrew went to see them, and based both on the band's sound and the crowd's reaction, he decided that he wanted to manage them. There was a gap in the British rock scene, and Andrew saw the Stones as being the band to fill it. After a few conversations with his partner, Eric Easton, they approached the Stones and made them an offer. On May 6, 1963, the Stones signed a three-year contract with Eric Easton and Andrew Oldham's new company, Impact Sound.

Now that the band was not on their own, new gates were opening up for them. Eric Easton was a long-time member of the show-business community, and as a former organ

The Rolling Stones

player, he knew many of the clubs outside of London. Booking the Stones in these would mean more exposure and a greater chance of reaching the same level of popularity as the Beatles.

One early sign of the new management's influence was the dismissal of Ian Stewart. Stu was a little older than the others (except Bill) and had a look that didn't match the hair and clothes of the others. Andrew felt that the band's image was just as important as their music, and he had a plan of how he wanted to present them. He wanted them to be like the darker side of the Beatles. Having a shorthaired guy playing piano simply would not do.

Although the entire band was against it, Brian broke the news to Stu that he would no longer be a full-time member of the band. He was told that he would be treated equally behind the scenes, but it was still an insult to a man who had been a part of the band since the beginning. As it would turn out, Stu would be an important part of the band until his death, but never as an up-front member.

On a Roll

The Rolling Stones, pictured here circa 1964, were touted as heavier and darker than their peers the Beatles.

Contracting a Contract

The next step for the Rolling Stones was to get a contract. British record companies were desperate to find a band to become the next big thing. One company in particular, Decca Records, was keen to find their big act. One of their talent scouts, Dick Rowe, had become

Drummer Charlie Watts, guitarist Keith Richards, and vocalist Mick Jagger backstage at a concert in January 1965.

On a Roll

famous as the man who turned down the Beatles, and he wanted to set things right. Dick ran into the Beatles' George Harrison one night, and George told him to check out the Rolling Stones. Not wanting to blow it again, Dick wasted no time. After going to see them play, Dick offered the boys a deal, and on May 14, 1963, Dick Rowe and Decca Records signed the Rolling Stones to a record contract. They had a steady lineup, a stream of live gigs, and now a record deal. The band was ready to go.

★3 Stone's Throw from Stardom

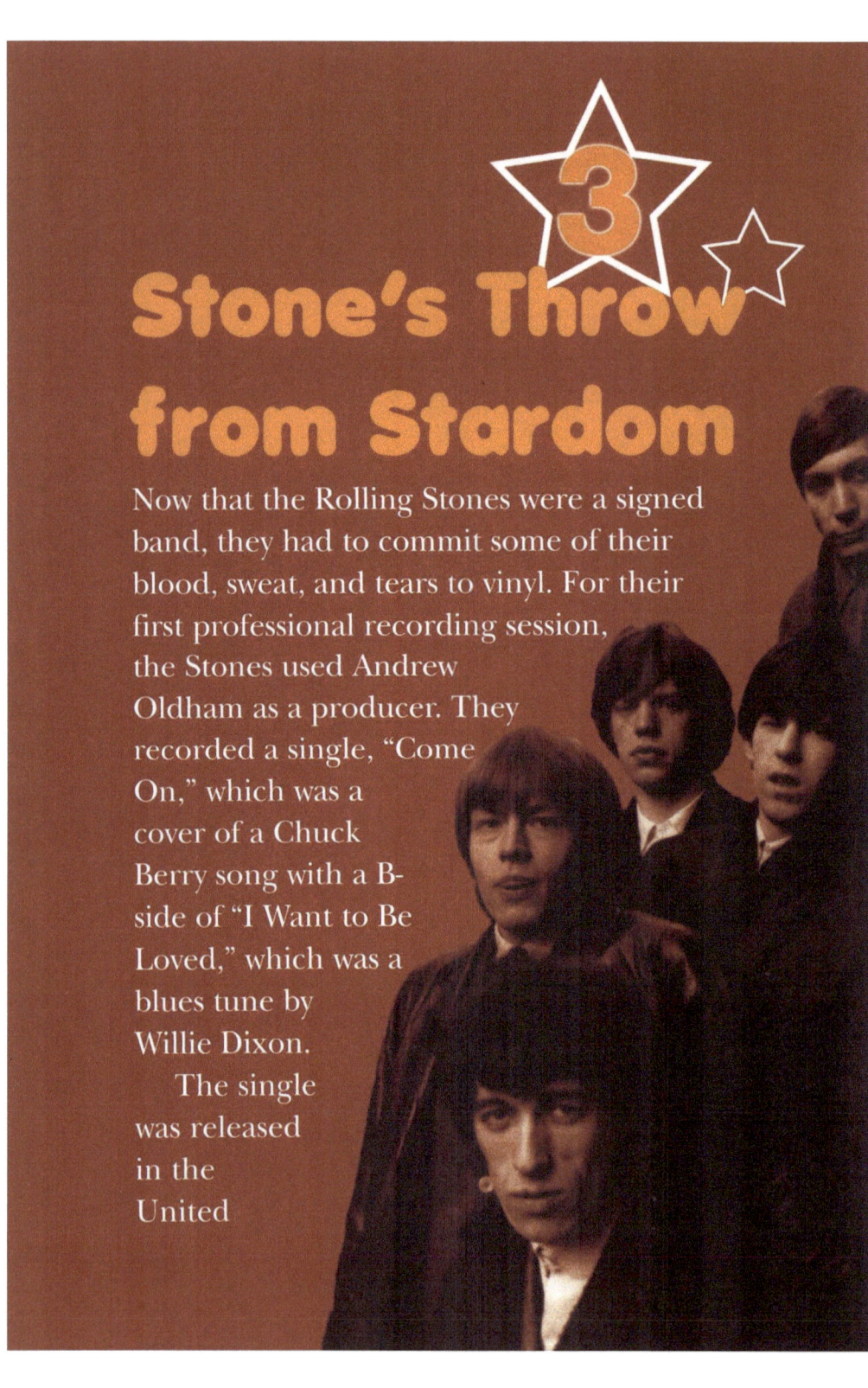

Now that the Rolling Stones were a signed band, they had to commit some of their blood, sweat, and tears to vinyl. For their first professional recording session, the Stones used Andrew Oldham as a producer. They recorded a single, "Come On," which was a cover of a Chuck Berry song with a B-side of "I Want to Be Loved," which was a blues tune by Willie Dixon.

The single was released in the United

Stone's Throw from Stardom

Kingdom on June 7, 1963. It was not an instant smash, but it floated around the middle of the top fifty for around three months. The Stones followed up the release of their single with their first appearance on British television, on a show called *Thank Your Lucky Stars*. Like the Beatles, they wore matching suits—but this style was quickly discarded. Tellingly, they played on the show without Ian Stewart.

The Stones Start Rolling

Hot on the heels of their single and television appearance, the Stones began rehearsing for their first national tour. They were to be on the bill with American rockers Bo Diddley and the Everly Brothers. One problem that they were starting to encounter, however, was Brian's health. He had always been asthmatic and had bad allergies, and as these conditions were acting up, he was starting to miss a show here and there. It wasn't about to stop them, but it certainly put a small handicap on things.

Another important step was made around this time. Andrew Oldham, always the smart

The Rolling Stones

businessman, understood that a band stood to make much more money if they wrote their own songs. Andrew urged Mick and Keith to start writing, but it had never occurred to the boys that it was something they could do. They were still playing and recording mostly covers, but the idea that they could write their own music was becoming more and more appealing.

They continued, for the time being, to play covers. On November 14, 1963, they began recording their first extended play (EP) release. It would consist of covers of American R & B songs. The EP, appropriately called *The Rolling Stones*, began climbing the charts as the Stones kept on touring. By the time 1964 began, they were on the road with the American girl group the Ronettes, and their EP was riding high at number two on the British EP charts. The single "I Wanna Be Your Man" was number nine on the singles chart.

In addition to the chart success, the Stones were starting to see their live audiences grow and grow, almost to the point where it was dangerous. Young women were rioting everywhere the boys

Stone's Throw from Stardom

played. At some gigs, the police would shut them down after just a few songs. Most of the time, the band would have to have a car waiting right near the exit to whatever club they played just so the boys could get out with their clothes and hair still attached. It was getting so bad that it moved Ian Stewart to say, "It wasn't pleasant to see what the music did to people."

Hide Your Daughters

In February 1964, just as their self-titled EP had hit number one on the EP charts, the popular rock magazine *Melody Maker* ran an article with the juicy headline "Would You Let Your Daughter Go With a Rolling Stone?" The title reflected what a lot of British parents were thinking at the time. Not only did most parents have no appreciation for the Rolling Stones' music, they also didn't like the appearance of the band. They were different from the Beatles in that the Stones had longer hair, looked dirtier, and played music that was rougher around the edges. While many English people proudly claimed the Beatles

The Rolling Stones

as one of their own, they spat on the Stones. This was Andrew Loog Oldham's plan all along.

Despite all the controversy, the Stones' careers were chugging along nicely. Their EP eventually reached number one, and they were busy recording their first full-length LP. On March 6, 1964, they finally released a single in the United States. A cover of Texas legend Buddy Holly's "Not Fade Away," it also included as a B-side the John Lennon/Paul McCartney song "I Wanna Be Your Man." They were still recording all covers, but Mick and Keith were starting to gain confidence as songwriters. They had already written a hit song for American rocker Gene Pitney, called "That Girl Belongs to Yesterday," but they had yet to record any of their own songs for themselves.

Beating the Beatles

On May 2, 1964, the Rolling Stones released their first full-length LP. Also called *The Rolling Stones*, the album came out in the midst of the band's increasing popularity. It shot to number one on the charts, ending the Beatles' year-long deadlock

Stone's Throw from Stardom

Did You Know?

Andrew Oldham wanted Keith Richards to use a sleeker name for the stage, so he adopted the shortened Keith Richard, like British rock superstar Cliff Richard. Up until the seventies, many of the Stones' albums credited him this way.

on top. The cover of the album, a simple photo of the band, was released without any words on it. No title or any other information was presented.

Striking while the iron was hot, and doing their best to capitalize on the popularity of British pop music, the record was released in the United States on May 29. Like so many other albums released in the United Kingdom first, it was re-titled. Called *England's Newest Hitmakers*, it shared with its U.K. counterpart the song "Tell Me."

The Rolling Stones

The Rolling Stones are greeted by well-wishing teenage girls after their June 1, 1964, arrival at Kennedy Airport in New York City.

The song is the first one written by Mick and Keith that was recorded by the band, but it would certainly not be the last. It seemed that anything the band put their minds to would happen. Now, of course, the latest challenge ahead of them was to tour the United States.

The Rolling Stones flew into New York's John F. Kennedy International Airport on

Stone's Throw from Stardom

June 1, 1964. They had only booked a nine-date tour, and they were not sure what to expect. After they crossed the country and landed in Los Angeles, California, they played their first show in the Swing Auditorium in San Bernardino, California. They were greeted by a youth riot to rival those taking place all over London, and the band was encouraged. Unfortunately, the next night in Texas, barely anyone showed up. They still weren't quite catching on all over the country.

One highlight of their U.S. tour was a recording session at Chicago's famed Chess Records. Chess had long been the home of down-and-dirty American blues, and for a group of young men who idolized the masters of this art form, it was a dream come true. As if the privilege of being allowed to record there wasn't enough, legendary bluesman Muddy Waters happened to be there when they came by. The Stones were shocked when the man from whom they'd taken their name graciously helped them carry their equipment.

The Stones pose for a group shot in New York City's Times Square during their American tour.

The Rolling Stones

Also on hand at Chess was rock superstar Chuck Berry, who had ignored the boys in past meetings. He arrived just as they were playing his "Around and Around," and couldn't help but compliment the Stones on the excellent job they were doing with his song. Recording at American studios was a practice the Stones would continue throughout their early career. America had been in the business of rock and roll much longer than the United Kingdom, and their producing and engineering techniques were far more advanced. Recording in the United States allowed them to get sounds that were impossible in their native land, and expert engineers like Chess's Ron Malo had the necessary experience to make a hot record.

Recording, Releasing, and Touring

The result of their Chess sessions was the album *12 X 5*, and on a second trip to America, they were booked on the influential *Ed Sullivan Show*. Sullivan was a TV host who had the power to make

Stone's Throw from Stardom

One of the first really big breaks for the Stones was their appearance on *The Ed Sullivan Show*, which gave them national exposure in America.

or break stars, and his high-rated TV show was the best way for bands to get exposure. The Rolling Stones played the show on October 25, 1964, to an ultra-enthusiastic fan response, both inside and outside the theater. Ed Sullivan was so flustered by all the screaming fans that he said the Stones would never be on his show again, which, veterans of his show realized, meant they definitely would.

The Rolling Stones

They also began their second U.S. tour around this time, trying to avoid some of the places where they had difficulty drumming up enthusiasm the first time. They had a single, "Time Is on My Side," doing well in the United States, and they found that the fans were multiplying every day in America.

One nagging problem, however, began popping up on the second American tour: Brian's health. Fragile as he was most of the time, being on the road only aggravated his condition further, and the Stones had to leave him behind in Illinois for a portion of the tour. They found themselves playing more and more without Brian, and Mick and Keith were writing more and more songs. Their albums, in fact, were containing fewer and fewer covers, and the balance of power within the band was starting to tip in their favor. Brian had founded the band, and he signed all the contracts for them and controlled the money, but he was rapidly finding himself losing control of the group.

Another tour difficulty for the Stones was the fact that rioting fans were popping up everywhere,

Stone's Throw from Stardom

not just at their concerts. Anytime someone found out which hotel the boys were staying in, they would be mercilessly hounded, and the hotel would inevitably be trashed by crazy teens. It got to the point where many hotels would not let the band stay there, and they would have to split up just to find places that would give them lodging. Even their transportation was getting trashed. When they couldn't get away fast enough, fans would tear their limos apart, even caving in roofs. It was getting insane, but the band had no choice but to roll with the punches.

Satisfied with Success

For the most part, the Stones were meeting with unqualified success on all fronts. In England, their new single "The Last Time" was number nine on the singles chart, and by February 1965, their U.K. album *The Rolling Stones # 2* was number one. They also continued touring England. By 1965, they had toured their homeland a total of seven times!

One thing they had yet to achieve in the United States, though, was a number-one

The Rolling Stones

single. On tour in America, Keith and Mick had been struggling to put a song together. They felt like they had something good, but it just would not take shape. Legend has it that Keith fell asleep one night and awoke to find that someone had recorded on his tape machine. When he played it back, he heard himself playing an incredible riff, which he must have done while almost totally asleep. The riff made its way into this new song, and they recorded it at RCA Studios in Los Angeles. The song was called "Satisfaction."

On June 4, 1965, "Satisfaction" was released in the United States first, and almost immediately it reached number four on the *Billboard* charts. Within weeks, it topped the charts, and by the time it was released in the United Kingdom, it had been number one for three weeks in the United States.

"Satisfaction" was by far the most popular song yet for the Rolling Stones. Its message tapped into what so many of the teens at the time felt about their square parents, teachers,

Stone's Throw from Stardom

and bosses. Its snarling dislike and confusion with the ways of the modern world were light-years removed from the classic teen love songs popular at the time. In addition, the music on the record was raw and savage, with the riff Keith had thought up in his sleep ripping through the rest of the music. In 2000, it was even named the best rock and roll song of all time by a poll of artists, producers, and journalists for a television special on the music channel VH1. The Stones had their first lasting classic.

★4★ Stones on Top

The Rolling Stones quickly followed up "Satisfaction" with the single "Get Off My Cloud," which was another hit. On July 30, 1965, London Records (the American subsidiary of Decca) released the new album *Out of Our Heads*, which was the first Stones album recorded entirely in the United States. It was also the first full album they released to go to

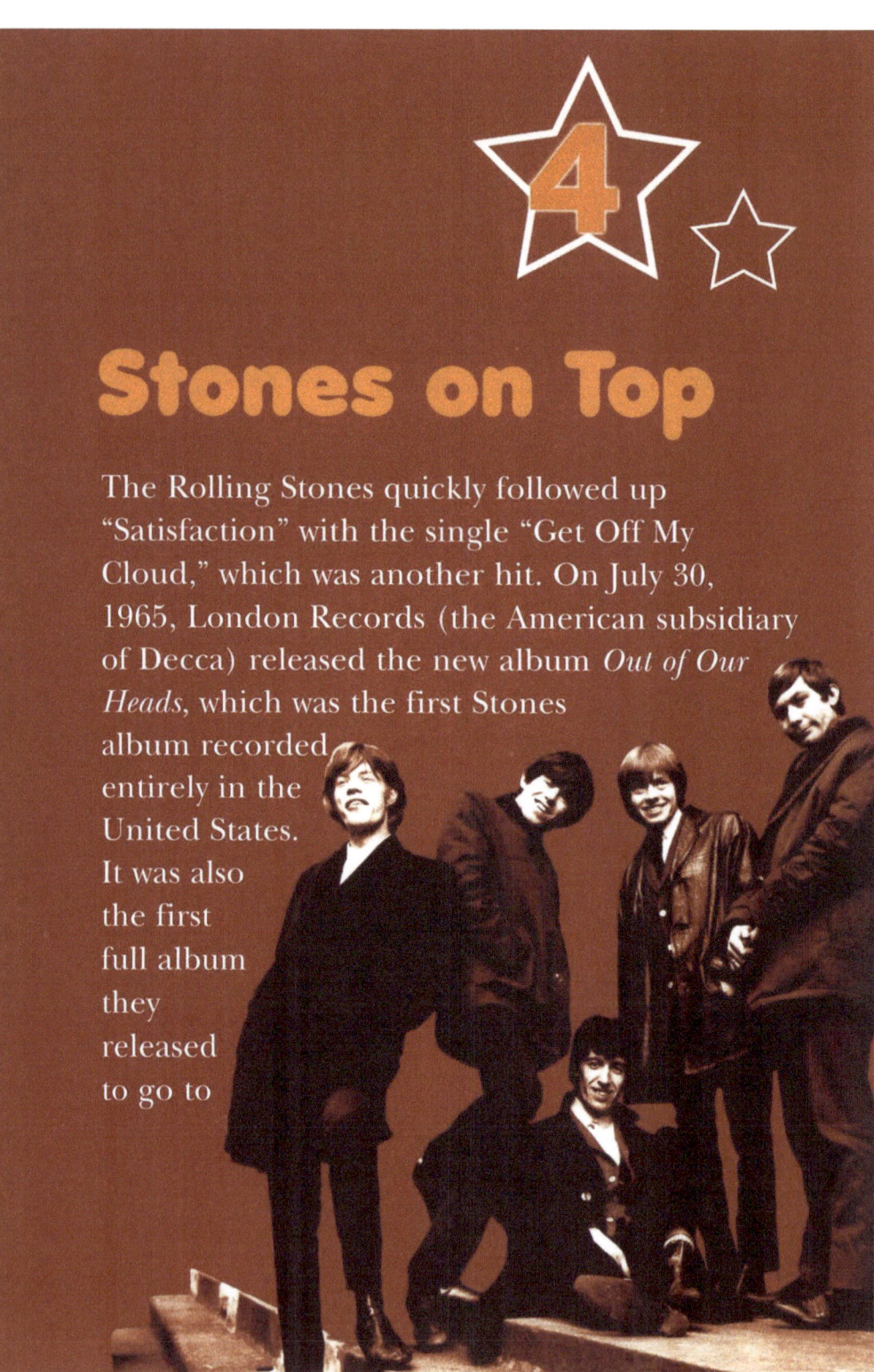

Stones on Top

number one in the United States. They could not have been hotter.

New Management

Now that the Stones were getting hot, they found that the heat was too much for their business manager, Eric Easton. For the most part, Eric's partner, Andrew Oldham, handled the creative development of the band, with Eric taking care of financial concerns. Things were quickly getting big for the Stones. With all that growth, they were looking for someone who could handle the big time.

They found their man in American accountant Allen Klein. Allen had made a name for himself as a record company auditor, and he had won artists, such as soul legend Sam Cooke, thousands of dollars that had been unfairly withheld from them by record companies. A New Jersey native, Allen wore unstylish suits, but he was a fierce and intelligent businessman. On August 28, the Stones signed a deal with Allen to make him and Andrew their official comanagers,

The Rolling Stones

With their newfound success, the Stones hired Allen Klein as their business manager.

with Allen running business from his New York office while Andrew controlled things from the road.

With new management in hand, the Stones continued to tour. They began their fourth tour of the United States, and this time "Satisfaction" had thrown them from the lower levels of fame into sheer superstardom. There were no more half-empty houses where they played, and their increased profile saw them making more money. Despite all the acceptance of their music by American youth, though, adults all over were still frightened and disgusted by the band. With Mick's hip shaking, the band members' long hair, and their sexually suggestive lyrics, they were seen as nothing less

Stones on Top

than the decline of Western civilization by many, which, of course, made kids love them more.

Aftermath of Success

The kids loved them so much, in fact, that in a month and a half of touring, the Stones made a staggering $2 million, putting them in the leagues of the very highest class of rock superstars. At the end of the tour, they continued their practice of recording while in the United States, again at RCA Studios in Los Angeles. This time, they set to work recording *Aftermath.* The first album that included only songs by Mick and Keith, it was as artistic and groundbreaking as any of the classic albums of the period.

The album's "Paint It Black" contained exotic Middle Eastern sounds and was unlike anything in rock and roll up to that point. Brian had learned to use the sitar (a stringed instrument from India with a long neck), and he used it on the song. It lent an air of mystery to the song and started the album with a bang.

The Rolling Stones

Elsewhere on the album, the Stones tried to live up to their reputation as surly bad boys, with seemingly cruel songs like "Under My Thumb" and "Stupid Girl." Not only did it make for some hair-raising rock, it also helped to set them apart from the friendly Beatles. The Beatles, it seemed, wanted to take you out for a soda and meet your parents, The Stones, on the other hand, sounded like they had different ideas.

The single "Paint It Black," despite being very progressive and forward sounding, went to number one. The year 1966 turned out to be a banner year for the Stones, with great record sales and steady sellout dates wherever they played. Brian, however, was losing more and more control of the group. His chronic asthma was becoming more of a problem, and it was becoming more apparent that Brian had a mounting drug problem. Also, he seemed more interested in traveling with his girlfriend, Anita Pallenberg, than working with the band. Mick and Keith were the ones creating all of the music, so it stood to reason that they would become the new leaders.

Stones on Top

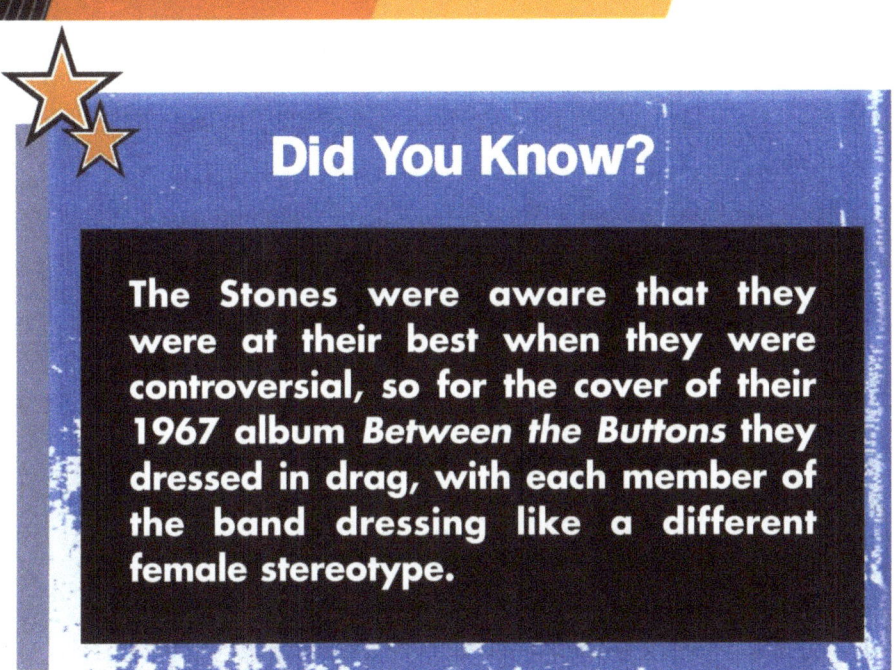

Did You Know?

The Stones were aware that they were at their best when they were controversial, so for the cover of their 1967 album *Between the Buttons* they dressed in drag, with each member of the band dressing like a different female stereotype.

1967

By 1967, Brian's involvement with the band was shrinking, and Mick and Keith were becoming first-class songwriters in league with heavyweights like John Lennon and Paul McCartney of the Beatles. There were many changes taking place for the band around this time, and at the end of the year, a whole new Rolling Stones would emerge.

The Rolling Stones

To start with, their album *Between the Buttons* was the last one that credited Andrew Loog Oldham as producer. He had been behind the boards for all of their recordings up until this point, but by this time, he was finding that they didn't need him anymore. On September 14, the band released a statement that they had officially parted ways with Andrew Loog Oldham, leaving Allen Klein as their sole manager.

Toward the end of that year, they released another album, *Their Satanic Majesties Request.* The sinisterly titled album was unlike anything the Stones had ever done, and without Andrew, they decided to simply produce it themselves. Stones purists did not like the album all that much and many critics thought it was confused sounding. Critics today believe, however, that it was a revolution in sound.

To many, it seemed like the Stones were trying to cash in on the popularity of the psychedelic sounds the Beatles had made popular with *Sgt. Pepper's Lonely Hearts Club Band,* and it looked like the Stones had really lost their sure footing. People thought they were too experimental and

Stones on Top

too different—they even had Bill Wyman singing lead vocals on one track! Today, as is often the case, the album is looked at as a fresh, original diamond in the rough, but at the time, it was a bit of a failure.

Not only were the Stones not seeing eye-to-eye with the public, tensions within the band were reaching a new high. Brian's girlfriend, Anita, had decided to run off with Keith, and the two band mates, who had once been like a right and left hand as guitarists, were no longer speaking. Now that Keith was not getting along with Brian, he and Mick were even closer than before, and it was crystal clear whose band the Rolling Stones was.

Recovery Records

Along with everything that had gone on with the band, the world itself was changing. The United States was getting more and more involved in the Vietnam War, and many of the young people who had come of age listening to the Stones had become politically active. It was clear to the band, especially after the so-so reception

The Rolling Stones

Rock and Roll Circus

The Rolling Stones' Rock and Roll Circus was a project designed for some of the finest rock and roll groups of the late sixties to strut their stuff. It was set up like a circus, complete with acrobats and animals. In between circus acts, bands like the Who, Jethro Tull, the Dirty Macs (John Lennon with Keith Richards, Yoko Ono, Eric Clapton, and Mitch Mitchell of the Jimi Hendrix Experience), and the Rolling Stones performed. Mick Jagger acted as the ringmaster.

After filming and editing, however, the project was mysteriously shelved until 1996. Rumor has it that the Stones were disappointed by their performance, and that they were embarrassed at being upstaged by an explosive performance by the Who. Whatever the real reason, the movie did not see the light of day for almost thirty years. Interestingly enough, this also marked Brian Jones's last public appearance with the band.

Stones on Top

The Rolling Stones' Rock and Roll Circus included artists such as Eric Clapton, John Lennon, and Yoko Ono.

their last album had gotten, that they needed to change with the times.

One of the first things they needed to do was get themselves a new producer. American Jimmy Miller, who had produced R & B acts like the Spencer Davis Group, fit the bill. They recorded a new single, "Jumpin' Jack Flash," with Miller and released it in May 1968.

The Rolling Stones

Anyone who thought the band was washed up after *Their Satanic Majesties Request* found that they were dead wrong. "Jumpin' Jack Flash" was one of the band's most powerful songs yet, and its harsh, rocking sound reflected the political turmoil going on all around them. They followed it up with another scorching single, "Street Fighting Man," which even more precisely spoke of the civil unrest going on all over the world.

The two singles were a teaser to the public for their next album, the universally respected *Beggar's Banquet*. This album brought the Stones right back to their roots and featured some of their earthiest blues yet. Songs like "Prodigal Son," "No Expectations," and "Factory Girl" were stripped down songs that sounded like they could have been recorded on someone's front porch, while the song "Salt of the Earth" celebrated the common man.

Elsewhere on the record, the Stones continued to stress their dark side. Nowhere was this more obvious than on the evil-sounding song "Sympathy for the Devil." The song itself was a meditation on evil throughout

Stones on Top

history and did not actually endorse Satanism. But the Stones played up their reputation as some serious bad dudes because it sold more records.

Brian's Sad Decline

While things had never been better for the band, they had never been worse for Brian. His health was declining. The woman he loved had left him for his band mate. He had run into trouble with the law, and was busted twice for drug-related crimes. And possibly worst of all, the very band he had started and willed into being had gradually eased him out of the spotlight.

That Mick and Keith were now the leaders of the group was undeniable, but what was in question was what Brian's role would be. At this point, he was just a lowly second guitarist. He was unhappy, and the band was unhappy with him. Also, the band had been away from the touring circuit since 1967, and they had a big tour planned for 1969. With his physical and mental health looking worse and worse, it was impossible for Brian to do the tour. It was definitely time for a change.

The Rolling Stones

Brian Jones, pictured here leaving court for a drug charge, was fired from the Stones in 1969.

The Stones had been recording some new material for their next album, *Let It Bleed*, and they had been looking around for someone to come in and jam with them. Toward the end of May 1969, they found a man named Mick Taylor, a former member of John Mayall's Bluesbreakers. At first, they didn't tell Taylor exactly what they wanted to meet up with him for, but he meshed well with the band while playing, and he was an excellent guitarist.

Shortly after meeting Mick Taylor, Mick, Keith, and Charlie went to Brian's farm in the English countryside. After a brief conversation, Brian was fired from the band he had started. They announced to the press that Mick Taylor would replace him. Taylor, only twenty years old

Stones on Top

and quiet, was the perfect replacement for Brian, as there was almost no danger of him trying to steal any of the spotlight from Mick or Keith, and he was good-natured and willing to cooperate.

Sadly, Brian's health problems were not the only threat to his well-being. On July 2, a friend staying at his country house discovered Brian floating in his swimming pool after taking a sleeping pill. By the time Brian was found, he was dead. To pay tribute to the man who had brought them together, the Stones played a free concert in London's Hyde Park on July 5, 1969. The concert had originally been planned as a chance for the public to get a look at the new Rolling Stones, and they were not sure if they should still do it. Unfortunately, this tragedy

The funeral procession for Rolling Stone Brian Jones, who drowned in 1969

63

Mick Jagger reads poetry in memory of Brian Jones, the Stones' deceased guitarist, at a memorial show in London's Hyde Park in July 1969.

Stones on Top

would not be the last tragedy of 1969 for the Rolling Stones.

Altamont: The End of the Sixties

The Stones were saddened by the loss of their friend, but they still had a lot of work to do. They had a new album, *Let It Bleed*, coming out, and they had a huge U.S. tour to support it. The tour was scheduled to take place throughout 1969, with a final, free show to be played somewhere in San Francisco at the end. The success of the Woodstock festival had made free festivals very hip, and the public wanted the Stones to do something similar.

The Rolling Stones decided to perform at the Altamont Speedway. The show's security was being handled by the local chapter of the famous biker gang, the Hell's Angels. The London chapter of the Angels had handled security successfully at the free Hyde Park show, and American Hell's Angels had been doing security for rock concerts for years without problems.

On the day of the show, December 6, it was obvious from the very start that something

The Rolling Stones

was wrong. During the set by one of the opening acts, Jefferson Airplane, the crowd started to get rowdy, and the Angels, who had come with pool cues and other homemade weapons, began beating people, including Jefferson Airplane member Marty Balin. By the time the Stones took the stage, tension between the crowd and the security had reached a boiling point.

While the Stones played, small riots were breaking out all over the grounds, and they were forced to stop their show several times while Mick urged people to "cool out." Finally, while the band played "Under My Thumb," one of the Hell's Angels stabbed a young man named Meredith Hunter. Hunter died, and the Stones barely escaped the riot that ensued.

Many people say that this marked the end of the feel-good late sixties. Woodstock had been about love and peace, but Altamont had turned into the exact opposite. The Stones, as a band, were born in the sixties, and had now provided a fitting closing chapter to the decade. Now, they had to find a way to survive into the next.

The Exiles

At the dawn of a new decade (and in the wake of Beatlemania), the Rolling Stones found themselves at the top, enjoying their immense popularity. But they also found themselves with a brand new set of challenges to overcome. Chief among those was the problem of their finances. The Stones had been making huge amounts of money through their touring and record sales, but they found themselves dependent upon their manager, Allen Klein, to give it to them. Allen controlled the money from the

The Rolling Stones

New York offices of Rolling Stones, Inc., and he had used much of it for his own gains. On July 30, 1970, the band announced the end of their relationship with Allen.

Also around this time, the band's contract with Decca Records ran out. Instead of re-signing with Decca, they decided to eliminate the middleman and create their own record company. This was a part of Mick Jagger's new plan for the band. He was working as hard as he could to fix the band's finances and organize their affairs, but he had an uphill battle ahead of him.

Sticky Situation

The first release the band put out on their Rolling Stones Records (with Atlantic Records distributing) was their 1971 album *Sticky Fingers*. It was yet another commercial and critical success, and proved that the band could function well without Brian. In many ways, recording the album was great for the band, as it was fun working with a new person, and it lent some fresh air to the process. *Sticky Fingers* continued with the dark

Bianca Perez Morena de Macias and Mick Jagger married in 1971.

The Rolling Stones

themes the Stones had been exploring, and the music was some of their finest.

Also in 1971, Mick Jagger, who had long been viewed as one of the hottest properties in the marriage market, was married to Bianca Perez Morena de Macias, a Nicaraguan socialite. Mick and Bianca's wedded bliss, however, was cut short by the cold hard facts of the Stones' tax bills. Faced with a huge amount of back taxes that they couldn't pay due to Allen Klein's financial mismanagement, the Stones had no choice but to leave their home country of England. After a goodbye tour of the United Kingdom, the band headed off to become citizens of the world. It seemed like a terrible thing, but it would end up leading to a huge creative breakthrough.

Exiles on Main Street

When the band fled England, Keith Richards set up shop in the south of France, in an exotic seaside villa. He also set up a recording studio downstairs, where he could lay down whatever sounds were coming out of his head whenever he

The Exiles

felt like it, which is exactly what he did. Throughout parts of 1971 and 1972, Keith would gather whoever was in the house at the time of inspiration and commit the music to tape. Mick was still very busy with his new marriage, so he recorded much of the vocals later on.

The method of recording in Keith's house led to an album with a clear version of Keith's style, the double album *Exile on Main Street*. With nothing but time on his hands, and the equipment literally right in his basement, Keith created a dense, multilayered record of raw, sloppy American blues and rock and roll. The songs are mostly about the tough life of a band on the road, and all are almost perfect in different ways. When it was released on May 12, 1972, critics and audiences alike were blown away by the quality of the songs and could not believe that the Stones and producer Jimmy Miller had topped themselves yet again. Since its release, in fact, it has been named as one of the greatest rock albums of all time, right alongside such modern sound revolutions as the Beatles' *Revolver* and the Beach Boys' *Pet Sounds*.

In the early 1970s, Mick, Keith, and the Stones, shown here during a 1970 concert in Rotterdam, reached new levels of creativity and financial independence.

The Exiles

Hot on the heels of the album, they began yet another giant U.S. tour. This time, they were in control of everything. They now had their own private jet, and nothing but the finest in everything. The tour gave them a chance to make some serious money now that no one was keeping it from them. As expected, it was another gigantic success, with opening acts like Stevie Wonder challenging the Stones to new heights of performance. Ten years after their formation, the Rolling Stones were at the very top of their game.

In the Soup

After setting such a high bar for themselves in 1972, 1973 was bound to look a little bit like a disappointment. Still, they went on to release *Goat's Head Soup*, the final of five albums with Jimmy Miller. There are many strong tunes on the album, most notably the mysterious ballad "Angie," but after something as powerful as *Exile*, almost any record would seem weak. The band also continued touring, this time doing a series of shows in the Far East and Australia.

The Rolling Stones

As it turned out, this would be the final tour for Mick Taylor.

Mick Taylor continued to contribute to the band, and he stayed on with them for all of 1973 and most of 1974 (during which they recorded yet another album, *It's Only Rock 'N' Roll*), but by the end of 1974, he had had it. The band was surprised, and in December they were supposed to record again, so Taylor's departure, which was made official on December 14, 1974, caught them off guard. They found themselves in the shaky position of finding another replacement. In public, though, they did not seem all that worried, with Mick making the remark, "No doubt we can find a brilliant 6'3" blonde guitarist who can do his own makeup."

A Stones Replacement

The last time the Stones needed a replacement guitarist, it was a secret affair. This time, however, it was well known, and everyone in town wanted the gig. The band was determined to take their time and make sure they had a replacement who

The Exiles

would fit in well with the band, especially Keith and Charlie, and who was used to the hard times of the road. They auditioned an endless string of seasoned players, but as soon as Ron Wood walked in, it was obvious he was their man.

Ron was a veteran of the British rock scene, having played with popular and influential British acts like the Faces, Rod Stewart, and Creation. He was also a close friend of Keith's, and Keith and Mick had both appeared on his solo album. Since he had been playing and hanging out with the guys for a while now, it was really no big deal for him to ease right into their routine.

Changing Times

The Stones got on with the business of breaking in Ron Wood with their 1975 U.S. tour. This tour was perhaps their most lavish yet, with a huge unfolding stage setup designed by Mick. The tour had them playing forty-five shows and was yet another smashing success, making about $13 million. They also swept year-end

The Rolling Stones

magazine polls, with magazines like *Creem* naming them best live band, best R & B group, and best group.

Mick and Keith, who were now producing for themselves under the name the Glimmer Twins, got Ron involved in the recording process. The first album with Ron, *Black and Blue*, was released on April 20, 1976. He had only become an officialmember in February of that year, but now he was fully in step with the band.

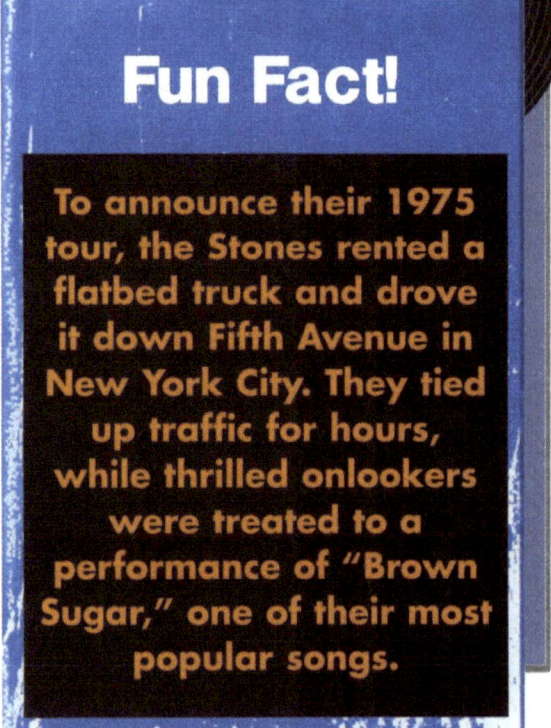

Fun Fact!

To announce their 1975 tour, the Stones rented a flatbed truck and drove it down Fifth Avenue in New York City. They tied up traffic for hours, while thrilled onlookers were treated to a performance of "Brown Sugar," one of their most popular songs.

The Rolling Stones play on the back of a truck driving through midtown Manhattan in New York City to publicize their 1975 tour.

The Rolling Stones

The Stones continued to roll with the times, but music was changing rapidly. The late seventies saw the explosion of punk rock, with loud, furious groups like the Buzzcocks, the Clash, and the Sex Pistols making the Stones' old style of rebellion look tired. At the same time, disco and new wave music were becoming popular, and it just didn't seem like old-fashioned rock had too much of a place anymore.

While they were still playing rock, they were unafraid to dip their toes into other styles. Their 1978 record *Some Girls*, for instance, contained "Miss You," a song with disco stylings. The record also featured a song called "Shattered," which bristles with punky energy. They also made a connection with the youth by agreeing to go on the hip young TV show *Saturday Night Live*. They played three songs and appeared in some of the comedy sketches.

Another place where they made some small changes was on their 1978 tour. This time, there was no complex stage setup, and instead of $15,000 designer outfits, Mick started wearing torn shirts and pants sealed with tape. They also

The Exiles

brought reggae legend Peter Tosh on tour with them, doing their best to expose people to another form of music. The Stones were entering their third decade, and they may have been rock dinosaurs, but they were not about to become extinct.

Start Up the Eighties

At the beginning of the eighties, the Rolling Stones were facing what seemed like an uphill battle. The pop charts began looking like an alien landscape, with skinny-tied new wavers and slick, modern R & B taking control. The Stones were still playing rough, blues-based rock and roll, despite a couple of experiments with other music, and it was hard to see them having a place in the new market.

They opened the decade with *Emotional Rescue*. It brought strong sales and fan reaction, and they began planning yet another U.S. tour, but

Start Up the Eighties

tragedy hit the band hard at the end of 1980. Their old friend John Lennon, of the Beatles, was shot dead in front of his apartment building in New York City. To many, it was a great loss, but to the Stones, it was the end of a long friendship. It also signaled the end of the time period from which the Stones came from. The Beatles had been broken up for ten years at that point, but with John dead, the Stones were now seen as British rock's great survivors.

Mick TV

For their new tour, the Stones accepted corporate sponsorship from Jovan, Inc., a cologne manufacturer, making it possible for them to launch a very elaborate and exciting show. At this point, the near-bankruptcy the band experienced at the start of the seventies was long gone. Allen Klein still controlled the legal rights for their 1960s music, but everything after that was theirs, and their constant touring had made them one of the richest acts in music.

Another important development that brought the Stones into a new age was the creation of

The Rolling Stones

the all-powerful MTV. With the Stones' video "Start Me Up," from their album *Tattoo You*, in heavy rotation at the start of MTV, they exposed themselves to a whole new generation of young people. They would continue their involvement with MTV, as well as VH1 to the present day, with Mick even giving out the Best Video Award at the 2001 MTV Video Music Awards.

The song "Start Me Up" first introduced kids to Mick's wild dancing, intense eyes, and expressive mouth, Keith's staggering guitar moves, and the Stones gained a whole new slew of fans. Their 1981 tour, despite the

Fun Fact!

On September 21, 1981, Mick Jagger, who had been denying everyone a face-to-face interview, did the only interview of this pre-tour period. Two junior high school girls, ages twelve and thirteen, from North Brookfield, Massachusetts, conducted the interview for their junior high newspaper!

Start Up the Eighties

changing face of music, was just as powerful a success as their previous tours.

Drifting Apart

Despite all of their success, the Stones were not as close as they once had been. After twenty years together, even the best friendships can wear thin, and people need to take a break. Mick Jagger and Keith Richards were no exception. The early eighties saw the boys in the band taking on different solo projects, getting married, and having children.

Bill Wyman and Ron Wood exchange guitar licks.

Keith married model Patti Hansen in 1983. Mick and Bianca divorced in 1980, and Mick became romantically involved with Jerry Hall, a Texas-born model-actress. Both Mick and Keith were welcoming new children into their lives. While they did release a new album,

The Rolling Stones

Keith Richards and fashion model Patti Hansen, pictured here in 1988, were married in 1983.

Undercover, in 1983, there was no sign of any new touring happening, and the band that had been releasing an album a year since the early sixties seemed to be slowing down.

In addition to spending time with their new families, both Mick and Keith were working on solo albums. Mick's first, *She's the Boss,* was released in 1985, and Keith's first, *Talk Is Cheap,* in

Start Up the Eighties

1987. Ron Wood had his own band, the New Barbarians, and Charlie Watts was playing big band music with his own orchestra. There were rumors floating around that the band was breaking up, and the truth is that Mick and Keith had been arguing quite a bit, but the band continued to find reasons to keep it together.

Stu's Final Bow

One such occasion for the band to play together came with some sad circumstances. On December 12, 1985, Ian Stewart, the piano player who had cofounded the band and been semi–kicked out, died of a massive heart attack. Stewart was only forty-seven, a fairly young age for a heart attack, and his death shocked the Stones. Despite being denied a front-row place in the band, Stewart had been with the band behind the scenes throughout their entire career. He had been playing piano for them, helping to organize their tours, and also serving to remind them where they came from.

Mick Jagger struts in front of a giant crowd at London's Wembley Stadium in 1982.

The Rolling Stones

The Stones had not played a concert together since their 1982 European tour, but they decided they had to do something for their fallen friend. On February 23, 1986, they played a private show at London's 100 Club for family and friends. Their set list did not include any Stones songs, but all classic blues numbers, exactly the type of stuff Stu would have wanted to hear. Losing him was a huge blow to the band, and with all of them following different impulses at the time, their future as a band looked bleak.

Wheels Keep Turning

Later on in 1986, the band released another album, *Dirty Work*, but again they did not tour to promote it. Instead, the band continued to rest, relax, and pursue their hobbies. Keith started touring with his new band, the X-Pensive Winos, Mick recorded with David Bowie and ultra-diva Tina Turner, and Charlie continued exploring traditional jazz and big band music. They say, though, that you can't keep a good man down, and the same goes for a good band. Toward the

Start Up the Eighties

end of the decade, in 1989, the Stones planned something huge for the public.

Since they had not toured at all since 1982, and had only really played together once since that time, public curiosity was high when they announced a brand new world tour. For the tour, they linked up with a promotional company called CPI (Concert Productions International), and they stood to make $70 million. To avoid the appearance that this would be a dusty oldies show, the band went back to the studio to record a new album, to be titled *Steel Wheels*. Now was the perfect time for the band to strike, as they were inducted into the Rock and Roll Hall of Fame on January 18, 1989 (by Pete Townshend of the Who). If ever there was an opportunity to remind the public that they were still a functioning, rocking band, this was it.

Even though the Stones had not been together much throughout the decade, they managed to put their personal interests aside to create some of their strongest music in years. They knew that they had a lot to prove, as the press was constantly mentioning their

The Rolling Stones

increasing age, and it would have been easy for them to come off as feeble old men trying to look young. On the tour, however, the questions of age were shattered as the band muscled through a two-hour-plus set every night.

The tour continued from North America on to Europe, with sell-out crowds every night. Suddenly, the Rolling Stones were red-hot again. There was so much demand for the band at the time, in fact, that much of the tour was recorded and filmed for a live album and video. The album, called *Flashpoint*, was released in 1991. It captures a band at the peak of their powers, a band who know each other's playing so well that it sounds seamless. With the close of the tour, the Rolling Stones found themselves wealthier and more popular than ever, and in the best possible position to enter their fourth decade, the 1990s.

Satisfaction

The Stones continued to build on the momentum they began with *Steel Wheels*. They followed up *Steel Wheels* with their live album, *Flashpoint*, and two more studio albums, *Voodoo Lounge* in 1994 and *Bridges to Babylon* in 1997. They also recorded an acoustic album, *Stripped*, in 1995, and they released another live album, *No Security*, toward the end of the decade.

They toured twice, once for *Voodoo Lounge* and once for *Bridges to Babylon*. Things

The Rolling Stones promote their *Bridges to Babylon* tour at a press conference under New York City's Brooklyn Bridge in 1997.

The Rolling Stones

continued along fairly normally, but not everything was the same. Perhaps the most important change was the exit of Bill Wyman. After thirty years with the band, in January 1993, he formally announced that he was leaving the group. Bill, who was considerably older than the other Stones, was simply tired of the rock and roll life. He was replaced by Darryl Jones, a younger bass player (but not yet an official Rolling Stone), and wrote a book called *Stone Alone*, which told all about his wild days with the band.

Another sad change the Stones had to deal with was the continuing loss of important friends and collaborators. Most devastating was the one-two punch of losing pianist Nicky Hopkins in September 1994 and producer Jimmy Miller in October. Through it all, the Stones quietly grieved and soldiered on, realizing that they were still doing what they were meant to do. Without Brian Jones, Ian Stewart, Bill Wyman, or any of the others, they were still the Rolling Stones.

Satisfaction

Jagger's Wandering Spirit

The nineties and beginning of the new century, however, did not only belong to the Stones as a band. Mick Jagger, now considered the definition of rock royalty, continued to follow his creative urges and dabble in other art forms.

But Mick Jagger, the rock god, is also a family man, and he had much to celebrate in the nineties. He became the first Rolling Stone grandfather when his daughter Jade had a child. He has also continued to explore his first love, music, releasing 1993's solo *Wandering Spirit*. He released another solo album in November 2001 called *Goddess in the Doorway*, which featured an all-star cast of guests including Pete Townshend and retro-rocker Lenny Kravitz. One track, "Joy," even features the ultra-popular U2 front man, Bono.

The Elegant Mr. Richards

Keith Richards has continued his romance with American rock and roll. He released his second

The Rolling Stones

Did You Know?

Mick Jagger started acting in films in the sixties, and he continued to do so in high-profile projects like *Freejack* (1992) with Emilio Estevez, and small art films like the concentration camp drama *Bent* (1999). In 2001, he even produced his first film, a World War II drama called *Enigma*, which had a strong showing at the Sundance Film Festival. He also acted in a new drama, *The Man from Elysian Fields*, with Andy Garcia and James Coburn.

solo album, *Main Offender*, on October 20, 1992, to outstanding reviews. Outside of the gloss of the Stones, Keith created a raw, soulful album of skeletal blues, with his ragged voice singing the truth. Never as commercial as his work with the

Satisfaction

Stones, Keith's solo records stay true to his blues roots (with an occasional detour into reggae country). He also guest-starred on singer-songwriter Tom Waits's album *Bone Machine* that same year, and the critics also greeted that album very warmly. It would seem that wild man Keith, who always had a bad reputation as a party animal, had become one of rock's most respected musicians.

2000 Men

The Stones as a band continue on into the new century. Their tour for *Bridges to Babylon* was one more success in a long line of them, showing the band's drawing power as being even more powerful than at the start of their career. Their fortieth anniversary tour will surely contain a string of sold-out shows—over the years the Stones have gathered an incredible number of fans.

And the Stones have not stopped coming up with new material. Spokesmen for the band have said that they are planning to record another album of all-new songs after the tour.

The Rolling Stones

Unfortunately, no one yet knows exactly when that will be. The amazing fact remains, though, that the forty-year-old band can still get it together to create new material and feel that they still have musical landscapes to explore.

Time Is on Their Side

The Rolling Stones have proven themselves to be the longest lasting rockers on the planet. Death, sickness, changing musical tastes, and even time

Concert for New York

On September 11, 2001, tragedy struck when planes crashed into the World Trade Center in New York City, the result of a terrorist attack. Many people in the entertainment community were left wondering what they could do to help. One event that was organized was the spectacular Concert for New York at Madison Square Garden. On

Satisfaction

Saturday, October 20, Mick Jagger and Keith Richards, along with A-list talents like David Bowie, the Who, the Backstreet Boys, Jay-Z, Billy Joel, James Taylor, and Paul McCartney performed. Much of the crowd was filled with people carrying signs for their lost loved ones and supporting the Fire and Police Departments of New York City.

Mick and Keith performed two songs, "Salt of the Earth," their tribute to the common working man from *Beggar's Banquet*, and "Miss You," from *Some Girls*. The concert, which was aired on the VH1 network, resulted in VH1's highest ratings ever and raised $30 million, which went to the Robin Hood Relief Fund to help people affected by the tragedy.

Mick and Keith on stage during VH1's airing of the Concert for New York, during which some of the biggest names in music pulled together to raise money for the families of the victims of the September 11, 2001, terrorist attacks.

The Rolling Stones

have been unable to stop them, and they show no signs of slowing down. Their body of work continues to catch the ear of new generations of music fans, and their faithful touring lets children and grandchildren (which, of course, many of the band members have themselves) hear what first made their parents and grandparents so excited when they were young.

Recent polls conducted on musicians, producers, and radio programmers for VH1 revealed that the Stones have four albums (*Beggar's Banquet*, *Let It Bleed*, *Sticky Fingers*, and *Exile on Main Street*) in the top hundred of all time. *Exile on Main Street*, in fact, ranked as high as number twelve. They were also voted the number-two artists in rock and roll history (behind, of course, the Beatles), and "Satisfaction" was voted the greatest song in the history of rock music.

Their legend is undeniable, but what is so interesting about the Rolling Stones at this point is not what they have done, but what are they are going to do next. One thing you can be sure of is that rock and roll's greatest survivors are far from finished.

SELECTED DISCOGRAPHY

1964 *England's Newest Hitmakers*
1964 *The Rolling Stones, Now!*
1964 *12 X 5*
1965 *Out of Our Heads*
1965 *December's Children*
1966 *Aftermath*
1967 *Between the Buttons*
1967 *Flowers*
1967 *Their Satanic Majesties Request*
1968 *Beggar's Banquet*
1970 *Let It Bleed*
1971 *Sticky Fingers*
1972 *Exile on Main Street*
1973 *Goat's Head Soup*
1974 *It's Only Rock 'N' Roll*
1976 *Black and Blue*
1981 *Tattoo You*
1986 *Dirty Work*
1989 *Steel Wheels*
1994 *Voodoo Lounge*
1995 *Stripped*
1997 *Bridges to Babylon*

GLOSSARY

asthmatic Having a disorder of the lungs that makes it difficult to breathe sometimes.
captivate To catch and hold attention.
conservative Not wild or overly extravagant.
controversy Something that causes disagreements and differences of opinion.
cover A song that has already been recorded by another artist.
elaborate Marked by being detailed or especially lavish.
engagement A scheduled date on which a band will play.
flustered Confused or taken aback.
mediocre Having qualities that are passable, but not especially good.
niche Someone's place in life.
psychedelic Experimental music that involves strange sounds and different song structures.
punk A style of rock featuring loud, raw music stripped down to the basics.

Glossary

riff Notes played on the guitar that are repeated throughout a song.

Satanism The practice of worshipping the Devil.

sinister Evil or menacing.

sitar A guitar-like, stringed instrument from India with a long neck.

suggestive Making one think of a certain thing without actually saying it.

turmoil Troubles or conflicts.

unqualified Without question.

Rock and Roll Hall of Fame and Museum
One Key Plaza
Cleveland, OH 44114
(888) 764-ROCK (7625)
Web site: http://www.rockhall.com

Rock and Roll Hall of Fame Foundation
1290 Avenue of the Americas
New York, NY 10104

Rolling Stones Fan Club USA
P. O. Box 2264
Cranberry Turnpike, PA 16066-1264
Web site: http://www.stonesplanet.com/usa.htm

To Find Out More

Web Sites

Due to the changing nature of Internet links, the Rosen Publishing Group, Inc., has developed an online list of Web sites related to the subject of this book. This site is updated regularly. Please use this link to access the list:

http://www.rosenlinks.com/rrhf/rost/

For Further Reading

Appleford, Steve, and Chris Welch. *The Rolling Stones Rip This Joint: The Stories Behind Every Song.* New York: Avalon, 2001.

Kallen, Stuart A. *The Rolling Stones.* San Diego: Lucent Books, 1998.

Phelge, James. *Nankering with the Rolling Stones: The Untold Story of the Early Days.* Chicago: A Cappella Books, 2000.

Works Cited

Booth, Stanley. *The True Adventures of the Rolling Stones.* New York: Vintage Books, 2000.

Karnbach, James, and Carol Bernson. *It's Only Rock 'n' Roll: The Ultimate Guide to the Rolling Stones.* New York: Facts On File, 1997.

Perry, John. *Exile on Main Street: The Rolling Stones.* Old Tappan, NJ: Macmillan Library Reference, 1999.

INDEX

A

Aftermath, 53
Altamont Speedway, 65–66
Avory, Mick, 25

B

Beatles, 8, 28, 29, 30, 33, 35, 37–38, 38–39, 54, 55, 56, 67, 71, 81, 102
Beggar's Banquet, 60, 99, 102
Between the Buttons, 55, 56
Black and Blue, 76
Bridges to Babylon, 91, 97

C

Chapman, Tony, 18, 23, 25
Chess Records, 41, 44
Concert for New York, 98–99

D

Decca Records, 31–33, 50, 68
Dirty Work, 88

E

Easton, Eric, 29–30, 51
Emotional Rescue, 80
England's Newest Hitmakers, 39
Exile on Main Street, 71, 73, 102

F

Flashpoint, 90, 91

G

Glimmer Twins, 76
Goat's Head Soup, 73

H

Harrison, George, 33
Hopkins, Nicky, 94

I

Impact Sound, 29
It's Only Rock 'N' Roll, 74

J

Jagger, Mick
    childhood of, 13–14
    dancing style of, 15, 82
    marriage/children of, 70, 71, 83–84, 95
    movie projects of, 96
    solo albums of, 84–85, 95
    as songwriter, 7, 36, 38, 40, 46, 48, 53, 55
Johns, Glyn, 6
Jones, Brian
    childhood of, 9–11
    death of, 63
    drug problems of, 54, 61
    fired from Rolling Stones, 62
    health problems of, 10, 35, 46, 54, 61

The Rolling Stones

Jones, Darryl, 94
"Jumpin' Jack Flash," 60

K
Klein, Allen, 51–52, 56, 67–68 70, 81
Korner, Alexis, 11, 14–15, 17, 18–19, 24, 27

L
Lennon, John, 38, 55, 58, 81
Let It Bleed, 62, 65, 102

M
McCartney, Paul, 38, 55, 99
Miller, Jimmy, 59, 71, 73, 94
MTV, 82

N
No Security, 91

O
Oldham, Andrew Loog, 28–29, 30, 34, 35–36, 38, 39, 51–52, 56
Out of Our Heads, 50

P
"Paint It Black," 53, 54

R
Richards, Keith
  childhood of, 11–13
  marriage/children of, 83–84
  solo albums of, 84–85, 95–97
  as songwriter, 7, 36, 38, 40, 46, 48, 53, 55
Rolling Stones
  appearance on *The Ed Sullivan Show*, 44–45
  early days/creation of, 6–7, 9–19, 22–33
  financial problems of, 67–68, 70, 81
  induction into Rock and Roll Hall of Fame, 89
  leadership of, 46, 54, 55, 57, 61
  lineup of, 17, 18, 22–27, 62–63, 74–75, 94
  naming of, 19
  reputation/image of, 27, 30, 37–38, 52–53, 54, 61
Rolling Stones, The (EP), 36
Rolling Stones, The (LP), 38
Rolling Stones # 2, The, 47
Rolling Stones Records, 68
Rolling Stones' Rock and Roll Circus, 58
Rowe, Dick, 31–33

S
"Satisfaction," 48–49, 50, 52, 102
Saturday Night Live, 78
Some Girls, 78, 99
"Start Me Up," 82
Steel Wheels, 89, 91
Stewart, Ian "Stu," 17, 23–24, 27, 30, 35, 37, 85–88, 94

Index

Sticky Fingers, 68–70, 102
Stripped, 91
"Sympathy for the Devil," 60–61

T

Tattoo You, 82
Taylor, Dick, 13, 14, 17, 18, 22, 25
Taylor, Mick, 62–63, 74
Their Satanic Majesties Request, 56, 60
12 X 5, 44

U

Undercover, 84

V

Vietnam War, 57
Voodoo Lounge, 91

W

Watts, Charlie, 6, 15, 24–27, 62, 75, 85, 88
Wood, Ron, 75, 76, 85
Wyman, Bill (Bill Perks), 6, 23–24, 26–27, 30, 57, 94

The Rolling Stones

About the Author

Thomas Forget is a writer, designer, and illustrator who lives in New York City. His father raised him to be a Rolling Stones fan.

Photo Credits

Cover, pp. 4, 7, 18, 26, 40, 45, 83, 84, 91, 92–93 © Corbis; pp. 5, 9, 12, 13, 16, 22, 28, 31, 32, 34, 42–43, 50, 52, 59, 62, 63, 64, 67, 69, 72, 77, 80, 86–87© Hulton/Archive/Getty Images; pp. 91, 100–101 © AP/Wide World Photos.

Series Design

Tom Forget

Editor

Eliza Berkowitz

Layout

Nelson Sá

www.ingramcontent.com/pod-product-compliance
Lightning Source LLC
Chambersburg PA
CBHW041112070526
44584CB00002B/143